SIX-MINUTE
NATURE
EXPERIMENTS

FAITH HICKMAN BRYNIE

Illustrations by Kim Whittingham

Sterling Publishing Co., Inc.
New York

To Tammy, Pete, and Cady

Edited by Jeanette Green
Designed by Judy Morgan
Copyedited by Margaret Dietz Denton

Library of Congress Cataloging-in-Publication Data

Brynie, Faith Hickman, 1946–

    Six-minute nature experiments / Faith Hickman Brynie ; illustrated by Kim Whittingham.

       p.   cm.

    Includes index.

    Summary: Provides instructions for simple science experiments, using everyday materials to explore weight, water, heat and chemistry, motion, botany, and the sun.

    ISBN 0–8069–9827–X

    1. Science—Experiments—Juvenile literature. 2. Scientific recreations—Juvenile literature. [1. Science—Experiments. 2. Experiments. 3. Scientific recreations.] I. Whittingham, Kim, ill. II. Title.

Q164.B9 1998

507.8—dc21   98-40851

1   3   5   7   9   10   8   6   4   2

Published by Sterling Publishing Company, Inc.
387 Park Avenue South, New York, N.Y. 10016
© 1999 by Faith Hickman Brynie
Distributed in Canada by Sterling Publishing
℅ Canadian Manda Group, One Atlantic Avenue, Suite 105
Toronto, Ontario, Canada M6K 3E7
Distributed in Great Britain and Europe by Chris Lloyd
463 Ashley Road, Parkstone, Poole, Dorset BH14 0AX, England
Distributed in Australia by Capricorn Link (Australia) Pty Ltd.
P.O. Box 6651, Baulkham Hills, Business Centre, NSW 2153, Australia

Sterling ISBN 0–8069–9827–X

Contents

Welcome

What a wonderful world we live in—full of mysteries and puzzles! Think about some of them. Days, months, and years go by in regular, predictable patterns as our vast planet moves through space. As seasons change, water freezes and melts. Rain falls, vanishes, then falls again. The Sun warms the earth. Winds whistle tunes in the air, steal your shouts, and cool your cheeks. Boats that weigh tons float on rivers and oceans. Machines whir and buzz and grind all around you, while green plants grow silent and strong through every crack in the sidewalk. Have you ever asked yourself how these things happen? Have you ever wanted to experiment to find answers for yourself?

If you said "yes," then this book is for you. These experiments invite you to have fun with the natural world—to find ideas and answers that were there all the time, just waiting for you to discover them. You'll work with what things weigh, how much space they take up, and whether they sink or float. You'll investigate some of the amazing tricks water can do, and you'll be hot on the trail of heat and cold. You'll do some crafty chemistry with rust and salt and ice that doesn't know when to melt. You'll make music, make things move, and encounter some life forms you may have never thought about before. You'll even have a chance to investigate the Sun, the Earth, and the seasons.

So open the book to any page and begin. As you experiment, think about what you are doing and why. What do you expect to find out? What changes do you see? What do your results mean? If you want to compare your ideas with what scientists say, you can turn to the Why-Oh-Why? section at the end of the book.

These experiments will help you appreciate how exciting nature really is. So welcome . . . and happy experimenting!

The KISS Method

Have you ever heard of the KISS method? It means "Keep it simple, silly." You can use the KISS method when you do the experiments in this book.

Don't make things complicated. These are simple experiments using simple materials. You don't have to work in a fancy laboratory to be successful. Don't worry if things don't turn out right the first time. You can always have another go. And don't worry about changing an experiment. You might even come up with something better.

Most of all, don't sweat the small stuff. If the experiment calls for tape, any kind will do. You don't need to turn the house upside down looking for a special type or run off to the store. This also applies to pans, bowls, cups, and other things. Something you find in your kitchen will probably work fine, even if it's not exactly what's shown. When a particular type of container is important, the experiment says so, sometimes giving both a description and a brand name.

Also, don't get hung up on measurements. Scientists usually measure solids in grams (g) or cubic centimeters (cc) and liquids in liters (l) or milliliters (ml). You'll see these quantities in parentheses for those who want to use the metric system. Don't let them confuse you or slow you down. Teaspoons and tablespoons from your kitchen are fine for measuring both liquid and dry materials.

Don't let temperatures confuse you either. Thermometers are labeled to show the system they use: an "F" (for Fahrenheit) or a "C" (for Celsius or Centigrade). Some thermometers show both. Scientists use the Celsius scale, but you can use either one. Just be careful to read from the same line of numbers every time you need to record a temperature.

And remember to take things one step at a time. A long experiment becomes a breeze, if you do it bit-by-bit. You can think about and learn from these six-minute nature experiments in your own way. Keep them simple and have fun!

part one

SOME WEIGHTY
Questions

A WAY TO WEIGH

There's no problem weighing big things. Just hop on the bathroom scale.

But what if you have something little to weigh and no scale for weighing it? Here's an easy way to compare the weight of small objects.

YOU NEED

⇒ tack or nail
⇒ scissors
⇒ rubber band
⇒ paper clip
⇒ small bulldog clip
⇒ toothpick
⇒ glue
⇒ ruler
⇒ masking tape
⇒ small plastic bag
⇒ 2 different kinds of pine-cones or other small objects

6

Let's Experiment!

1. Ask an adult if there's a place on a wall, bulletin board, or doorjamb where you can safely put up a tack or nail. Put it just above eye level.

2. Cut the rubber band. Tie one end to a paper clip.

3. Put a drop of glue along the inner, rounded surface of the bulldog clip (between the pincers). Put the toothpick in so that its points stick out on both sides.

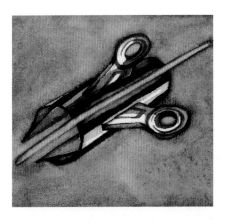

4. Tie the other end of the rubber band through the pincers of the bulldog clip.

5. Hang the paper clip from the tack.

6. Tape a ruler upside down and vertically alongside, so that the bottom of the paper clip lines up with 0 (zero) and the toothpick points to the numbers.

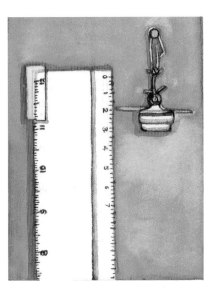

7. Put a pinecone or other small object in the plastic bag. Hang it from the bulldog clip. Read the number the toothpick points to. Write the number down.

8. Remove the first object from the bag and put in the second. Hang the bag from the bulldog clip. Read the new number. Which object weighs more? How do you know?

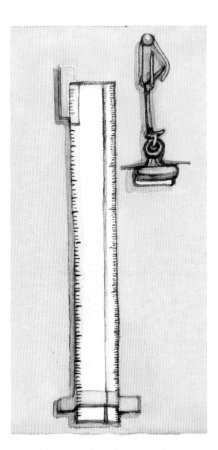

WANT TO DO MORE?

Use this way to weigh in these experiments:

Fun's A-Poppin', page 8

The Freezin' Season, page 18

Wet, Wetter, Wettest, page 21

Slim-sulation One, page 27

One-Way Waterway, page 38

Handy Hints

☞ For greatest accuracy, measure in millimeters or in sixteenths of an inch.

☞ Attach the bag at its center so the toothpick hangs level.

RIGHT   WRONG

Why-Oh-Why?

Have you ever wondered what "weight" actually means? Get some heavy ideas on page 72.

FUN'S A-POPPIN'

Harold and Harvey are fighting about who has more popcorn. Harold says he has more because his carton is bigger. Harvey says his corn weighs more. Do this experiment to find out who's right.

YOU NEED

⇒ bag of microwavable popcorn and microwave oven OR

⇒ plastic bag

⇒ measuring cup

⇒ ¼ cup (70 g) of popcorn

⇒ air popper for popcorn (no oil)

⇒ Way to Weigh scale, page 7

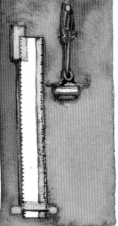

Let's Experiment!

1. If you have not already made one, build the Way to Weigh scale, page 7.

2. If you are using a microwave oven, skip to step 5. If you are using a popcorn popper, put ¼ cup (70 g) of unpopped corn in the plastic bag.

3. Attach the bag to the bulldog clip and read the number beside the toothpick. Write the number down.

4. Pop the corn. Let the popcorn cool a little. Then put it in the bag, clip it to the rubber band, and read the number beside the toothpick again. Skip to step 7.

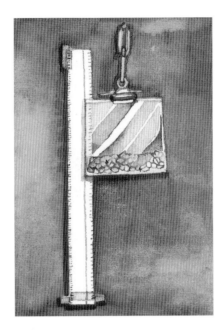

5. Clip the bag of microwavable popcorn to the scale. Read the number beside the toothpick.

6. Pop the corn in the microwave. Let it cool for a few minutes, then clip the bag to the rubber band and weigh it again.

7. Which weighs more—the popped or the unpopped corn? How do you know? What explains the difference?

WANT TO DO MORE?

⇒ Try the same experiment with cooked and uncooked vegetables. Or try weighing an apple slice, drying it, then weighing it again.

⇒ Weigh ten raisins. Soak them overnight, then weigh them again.

⇒ Weigh a ball of firm cookie dough. Bake the dough and weigh the finished cookie.

Why-Oh-Why?

Weight can't be seen, but it can disappear. How can that happen? Pop over to page 72 to find out.

Handy Hints

☞ Be sure to follow the instructions on the package when popping corn.

☞ Be careful not to burn your fingers when opening a bag of microwaved popcorn.

THAT SINKING FEELING

Captain Courage is sailing the high seas with a fortune in spices. If his ship swamps in a squall, he's got a sinking feeling he knows which part of his cargo will end up on the bottom. Do you?

YOU NEED

⇒ water

⇒ vegetable oil

⇒ 1 teaspoon (5 cc) ground black pepper

⇒ 1 teaspoon (5 cc) dried *minced* garlic (not garlic powder)

⇒ measuring spoon

⇒ 3 jars with lids

⇒ measuring cup

Let's Experiment!

1. Add equal amounts of water and oil to each jar.

2. To one jar, add the black pepper. To another, add the minced garlic. Add nothing to the third.

3. Put the lids on the jars. Shake them all vigorously. Then let them sit for 30 minutes.

4. After 30 minutes, describe what you see. Where is the pepper? Where is the garlic? What happens to the oil and vinegar? Can you explain why?

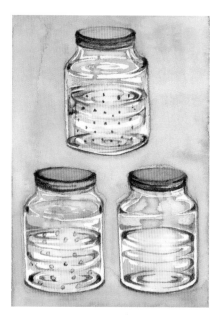

WHAT'S NEXT?

Try the same experiment with other dried spices. If you've got a sinking feeling you know what's happening, turn to page 72 to see if your ideas will float.

A COTTON TALE

What tales can cotton balls tell about sinking and floating?

YOU NEED

⇒ 2 cotton balls
⇒ vegetable oil
⇒ glass
⇒ pan or sink of water

Let's Experiment!

1. Pour a little vegetable oil into a glass. Add one cotton ball. Turn it until its outside is covered in oil.

2. Put both cotton balls in water. Watch what happens. Try to explain what you see.

WHAT'S NEXT?

Do any other liquids have the same effect as the oil? Try some and see. Then cotton on to the explanation for what you saw by turning to page 72.

BOATLOADS

If two boats are the same size, will they float, no matter what their loads are? Try this experiment and see.

YOU NEED

⇨ two 35-mm film canisters
⇨ vegetable oil
⇨ corn syrup
⇨ pan or sink of water

Let's Experiment!

1. Fill one canister with vegetable oil. Fill the other with corn syrup.

2. Carefully seal both so that no air is trapped inside.

3. Put both canisters in water. What happens? Why?

WHAT'S NEXT?

Try filling the canisters with vinegar, water, sand, or something else. What happens? Then row on over to page 72 for ideas about sinking and floating.

WHEN'S A BOATFUL NOT A BOAT, FULL?

*M*elvin's boat is carrying 5,000 passengers—all of them toads. The boat will travel from Lake Erie along the St. Lawrence Seaway. Then it will cross the Atlantic Ocean to London. (Don't worry about the toads. They've been on vacation in Ohio and are returning home to Soho.)

The toads have only one question. Where will the boat be safer—in the freshwater lake or on the salty sea? Try this experiment to help the toads find the answer.

YOU NEED

⇒ small, round balloon

⇒ 1-cup measuring cup made of glass

⇒ water

⇒ measuring spoons

⇒ 2 tablespoons (30 cc) of salt

⇒ spoon

Handy Hints

☞ Don't inflate the balloon. It won't fit in the cup.

☞ Stretch the neck of the balloon several times to make it easier to tie.

Let's Experiment!

1. Pour a small amount of water into the balloon—enough to fill it without inflating it. Tie it off tightly.

2. Measure ½ cup (125 ml) of water into the measuring cup. Put the balloon in the water.

3. Where is the bottom of the balloon? Read the water level on the side of the cup. Write down how high it is.

4. Remove the balloon. Add the salt to the water and stir until nearly all the salt dissolves.

5. Return the balloon to the water. Where is the bottom of the balloon now? Where is the water level?

WANT TO DO MORE?

⇒ Put a little corn syrup in the balloon and repeat the experiment. Are the results the same?

Why-Oh-Why?

Now can you tell the toads where Melvin's boat might sink? Sail over to page 72 to see if your ideas hold water.

p a r t   t w o

WHAT ABOUT

Water?

• •

ALL PUDDLED-UP

It rained barrelfuls last night, and now the streets and ditches are dotted with puddles. Some are deep and narrow. Some are wide and shallow. Soon the Sun will come out and the puddles will disappear. Do you know where the water goes?

Think of an answer to that question while you experiment to see which dry more quickly—deep puddles or shallow ones.

YOU NEED

⇒ clean, empty soup can

⇒ clean, empty tuna can

⇒ measuring cup

⇒ water

⇒ ruler

⇒ piece of construction paper

⇒ scissors

⇒ tape

⇒ clock or watch

⇒ sunny spot to work in

Let's Experiment!

1. Measure ¼ cup (60 ml) of water into each can.

2. Cut a strip of construction paper the same length as the ruler. Tape the paper to the back of the ruler. *Tape at the top only.*

3. Put the ruler into the water in one can. Make sure the ruler is straight up and down and the 0 (zero) end points down. When you pull the ruler out, the construction paper will be wet. Read the ruler at the wet mark. This is the depth of your puddle.

4. Discard the wet construction paper, dry the ruler, and put on a new

piece of dry paper. Repeat the depth measurement in the other can.

5. Place both pans together in a sunny spot. Note the time.

6. Use fresh pieces of paper to measure the depth of the water in both cans every 30 minutes.

Keep measuring until one puddle dries up. Which disappears first?

7. Make a graph of your results like the one on page 16. Put time along the bottom, depth along the side. Plot points and draw a line for each of your puddles.

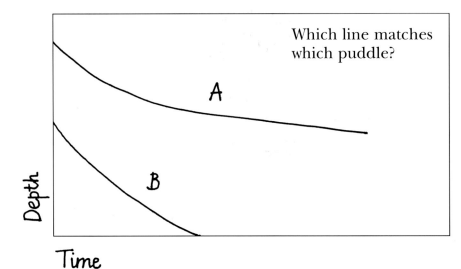

Which line matches which puddle?

A

B

Depth

Time

Why-Oh-Why?

Puddles don't disappear by magic. The water goes somewhere, but where? And why does it take numbers to explain how fast puddles dry? Look for some in-depth answers on pages 72 and 73.

WANT TO DO MORE?

⇒ In cans of different sizes, make puddles that are *all the same depth*. Which dries first?

⇒ Find out if puddles of salt water dry as fast as freshwater ones.

⇒ Do puddles dry faster in sunlight or in shadow? Experiment to find out.

Handy Hints

☞ Why do your containers have to be made of the same material? Would it be fair to test a shallow puddle in a glass jar against a deep puddle in a tin can?

☞ If you want to speed up the experiment indoors, try putting your puddles under a hot lamp. Can you guess why this works?

RAIN, MAN!

It hasn't rained in Dull Gulch Desert since Bernie was a pup, but Riley the Rainmaker claims he can change things. Can he? Let's find out.

16

YOU NEED

⇒ 2 tall glasses

⇒ 3 ice cubes

⇒ 2 plastic sandwich bags

⇒ 2 rubber bands

⇒ hot water

⇒ cold water

Let's Experiment!

1. Fill one glass one-third full with cold water and an ice cube. Fill the other glass to the same level with hot water.

2. Put an ice cube in each sandwich bag.

3. Fit the bags over the tops of the glasses so that the ice cubes hang inside. They should not touch the water below. Hold the bags in place with rubber bands.

4. Watch what happens over the next 30 minutes.

Look for answers to these questions:

⇒ What *two* things happen on the *inside* of one glass but not the other?

⇒ What *one* thing happens on the *outside* of one glass but not the other?

⇒ How can these things be explained?

WANT TO DO MORE?

⇒ Leave a glass in the freezer for a while. Then take it out and let it sit in a warm place. What happens? Why?

⇒ Fill a coffee can with a mixture of crushed ice and salt (about 2 parts ice to 1 part salt). Wet some newspaper and set the can on it. Wait a while to see what happens on the side of the can and what happens to the paper.

Handy Hint

☞ This experiment works best in a warm, damp room. Can you guess why?

Why-Oh-Why?

Riley the Rainmaker is waiting for your advice. Drizzle over to page 73 for an idea of what to tell him.

T[HE] FREEZIN' SEASON

Winter in the Far North, and it seems all the water in the world has shrunk into ice. Water does shrink when it freezes, doesn't it?

YOU NEED

⇒ rain gauge (from a garden shop or hardware store)

⇒ measuring cup

⇒ water

⇒ unbreakable glass

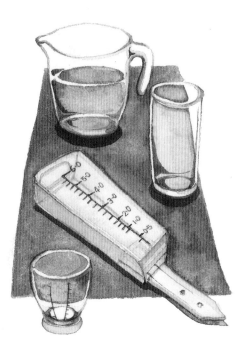

Let's Experiment!

1. Put the rain gauge in a glass so that it stands straight and level. If you don't have a rain gauge, you can use a measuring cup, but the results won't be so easy to measure accurately.

2. Pour water into the gauge exactly to the 4-inch or 100-mm mark.

3. Put the glass and gauge in the freezer. Leave them overnight. The next day, remove them from the freezer. Read the level in the rain gauge. What's going on?

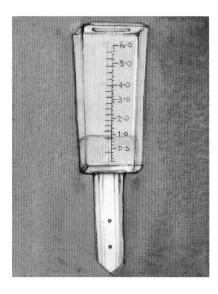

WHAT'S NEXT?

Outside in the winter, collect snow in the rain gauge. Read the level. Bring the gauge inside and let the snow melt. Read the level again. Try to explain what you've seen. Then turn to page 73 for the facts about freezing.

SOAP BOATS

Higgy and Henny are taking no chances. They want to be sure their boat will get them home, so they've got a sail, oars, and a motor for power.

They know a boat can't skim across the water all by itself. Or can it?

YOU NEED

⇒ two 6-inch (15-cm) square pieces of aluminum foil

⇒ tracing paper

⇒ pencil

⇒ scissors

⇒ few drops of dishwashing liquid

⇒ water (in a bathtub)

⇒ masking tape

⇒ measuring tape

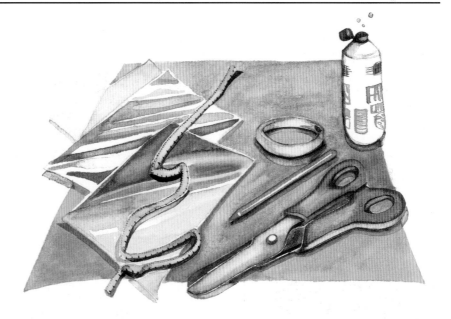

Let's Experiment!

1. Trace the two shapes on page 20 onto the tracing paper, then onto the foil.

2. Cut out the shapes to make two boats.

3. Run cold water, about 2 inches (5 cm) deep, into a bathtub.

4. Float the boats on the water at one end of the tub. Mark your starting line with a piece of masking tape stuck to the side of the tub.

5. With the boats at the starting line, drop a single drop of dishwashing liquid into the round holes. See page 20. Watch what happens.

6. Use the measuring tape to measure how far each boat travels before it stops. Which travels farther? Which travels faster?

Handy Hint

☞ The water must be soap-free for the boats to sail. Use fresh, clean water each time you try a new boat.

WANT TO DO MORE?

⇒ Improve your boat's design. Try different shapes. Try different sizes and positions for the holes.

⇒ Compare boats made of different materials. Try index cards, file folders, vinyl sheets, or plastic-coated paper.

⇒ Compare different liquids. Try bubble bath, hand soap, body lotion, and others you find around the house.

Why-Oh-Why?

The soap boat has no sails, no oars, and no motor—but it goes. What makes it travel? Skim over to page 73 for some answers.

WET, WETTER, WETTEST

It's one thing to be wet. It's another to get soaked, drenched, or drowned! Do some things get wetter than others? Here's a fun way to find out.

YOU NEED

⇒ 3 or more paper towels of different brands

⇒ scissors

⇒ bowl

⇒ water

⇒ Way to Weigh scale, page 7

Let's Experiment!

1. If you have not already made one, build the Way to Weigh scale, page 7.

2. Cut all the paper towels to the size of the smallest towel.

3. Clip one dry towel to the Way to Weigh scale. Write down the number beside the toothpick pointer.

4. Put some water in a bowl. Put in the paper towel. Let it get completely wet.

5. Pull out the towel and hold it above the water until it stops dripping. *Don't wring or squeeze.*

6. Clip the towel to the Way to Weigh scale again, and record the new number.

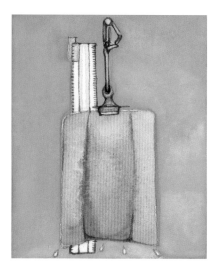

Towel	Dry (mm)	Wet (mm)	Diff (mm)
Springy	73	97	?
Wettums	65	....	?
Wipems	....		?

7. Repeat steps 3 to 6 for each towel. Write down all your numbers in a table, so you can compare them.

8. Which towel absorbs more water? How do you know?

WANT TO DO MORE?

⇒ Try the same experiment with samples of different fabrics, such as cotton, silk, or denim.

⇒ Try the same experiment with oil instead of water.

⇒ Become a consumer research scientist. Do experiments that will tell shoppers which is the best brand of paper towel to buy. Think of a way to make the price of the towel a part of your recommendation.

Handy Hint

☞ For a fair test, all the paper towel pieces must be the same size. Do you know why?

Why-Oh-Why?

A paper towel can soak up water, but how? Why can some towels hold more water than others? Get absorbed in the answers, page 73.

part three

HEAT AND COLD

A HEAT WAVE

"It's a scorching heat wave," says weatherman Tim. *"The mercury is really soaring."* What's Tim talking about? Build a thermometer and see.

YOU NEED

⇒ aluminum soft-drink can (pull-tab type, empty)

⇒ see-through drinking straw

⇒ food coloring

⇒ clay

⇒ paper towel

⇒ bowl

⇒ water

Let's Experiment!

1. Put three drops of food coloring in the empty soft-drink can. Fill it with cold water all the way to the top.

2. Put the straw through the hole in the top of the

23

can. Dry the top with a paper towel.

3. Seal around the straw with clay. Seal tightly. *No leaks.*

4. Fill the bowl with hot water and set the can in it. Watch the colored water inside the straw. What happens?

5. Remove the can from the bowl. Discard the hot

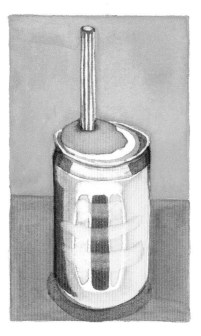

water. Replace with cold water. Put the can back in.

6. What happens now? Can you explain why?

WHAT'S NEXT?

The liquid inside a thermometer rises on a hot day and falls on a cold one. Put the thermometer you've built outside and see what happens. Then turn to page 73 to find out why.

THE GREENHOUSE EFFECT

Gardeners know that seeds sprout sooner in a greenhouse than they do if planted outside. What's happening under that greenhouse's glass roof? Try this experiment to find out.

YOU NEED

⇒ 2 flexible temperature strips, or liquid crystal thermometers (from an aquarium supply store)

⇒ tape
⇒ piece of white paper
⇒ glass
⇒ bright lamp (gooseneck is best)

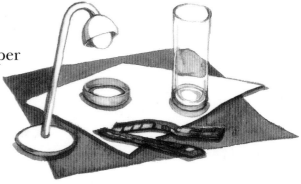

24

Let's Experiment!

1. Tape the temperature strips into circles, with the numbers on the outside. Place them on the paper.

2. Put the glass over one strip. Leave the other as it is. Turn on the lamp.

3. Wait 20 minutes. (Longer, if the lamp is dim or high above the strips.) Read the temperature on both strips. How do they compare?

4. Which one is hotter? Why?

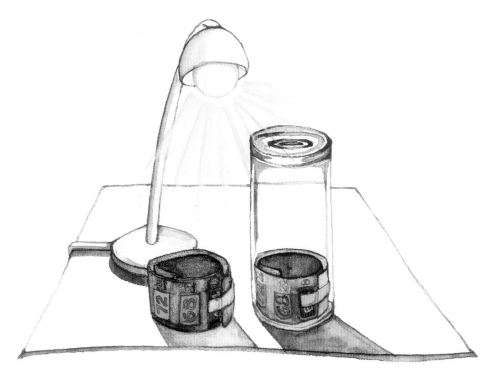

WHAT'S NEXT?

Is this "greenhouse effect" always a good thing? On pages 73 and 74 read about how pollution and the greenhouse effect threaten the Earth's climate.

HOT COLORS

Henny lives at the North Pole, and she's FREEEEEEEZING. She wants to know what color of coat to buy. After you finish this experiment, you'll be able to tell her.

YOU NEED

⇒ 2 aluminum soft-drink cans (pull-tab type, empty)

⇒ piece of black paper

⇒ piece of white paper

⇒ scissors

⇒ tape

⇒ ruler

⇒ 2 glass or plastic, rigid aquarium thermometers (range: to about 40° C or 100° F or higher)

⇒ modeling clay

⇒ bright lamp (gooseneck is best)

Let's Experiment!

1. Cut a strip of black paper and a strip of white paper 5 inches (13 cm) wide and 11 inches (28 cm) long. Tape the black paper strip around one can and the white paper strip around the other can.

2. Some aquarium thermometers have suction cups at the bottom. Remove them. Put the thermometers through the holes in the tops of the cans. Use clay to hold the thermometers in place. *You should be able to see, above the clay, the top of the column of liquid inside each thermometer.*

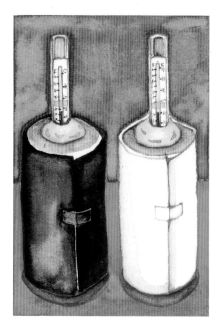

3. Set the cans about 2 inches (5 cm) away from the lamp.

4. Read the temperature in each can. Write down the number.

5. Turn on the light. Wait ten minutes. Then read the thermometers again.

6. Has the temperature inside the cans changed? Has one changed more than the other? Can you explain why?

WANT TO DO MORE?

⇒ Try the same experiment using different colors, such as red, green, or yellow.

⇒ Repeat the experiment, but this time fill the cans with water. You'll need several hours to see much difference.

⇒ In hot weather, put blown-up black and white balloons in a sunny spot. Which pops first?

⇒ In cold weather, put blown-up black and white balloons outdoors. What happens?

Handy Hints

☞ The temperature inside the two cans should be the same when you begin, but thermometers can vary. Make sure you read both before turning on the light.

☞ Many aquarium thermometers have two scales: a Fahrenheit (° F) scale and a Celsius (° C) scale. Scientists always use the Celsius scale. You may use either one. Just make sure you don't mix them up.

Why-Oh-Why?

Can you tell Henny what color of coat will keep her warm at the North Pole? Too late. She's moved to the tropics. Now she's ROOOOOOASTING, and she wants to know what color to paint her house. Can you help her? For a hot tip on some cool colors, turn to page 74.

SLIM-SULATION ONE

Ah, nothing's more refreshing than a cold drink on a hot day, but good things never seem to last. The ice keeps melting. Is there any way to stop it . . . or at least slow it down?

INSULATORS are materials that keep hot things hot and cold things cold. Some are slim insulators. They keep out the heat and are light-weight, too.

Experiment with insulators to see which are best at keeping your ice icy-cold.

⇒ 4 or more zip-top sandwich bags

⇒ measuring cup

⇒ water

⇒ 3 or more samples of possible insulators, such as newspaper, cardboard, plastic wrap, aluminum foil, fabric, fake fur, a winter scarf or glove.

⇒ Way to Weigh scale, page 7

Let's Experiment!

1. Measure ½ cup of water into each of four zip-top sandwich bags. Seal the bags and freeze them overnight.

2. Do your experiment in a warm place. Take the bags out of the freezer. Leave one exposed to the air. Wrap the others in the insulating materials you want to test.

3. Check the unwrapped bag every 20 minutes. When the ice appears to be about half melted, open the bag and pour off the water.

4. Weigh the ice that's left on your Way to Weigh

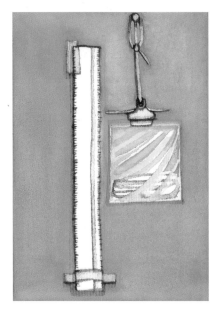

scale. Record the number that the toothpick points to.

5. Open the remaining bags, pour off the water, and weigh the ice in each. Record your numbers as in the table above.

6. Which material is the best insulator? How do you know?

Material	Wt. # (mm)
None	76
Mitten	96
Foil	

WANT TO DO MORE?

⇒ Suppose you wanted to keep things cold on a rocket ship. You'd want a good insulator that weighed very little. Test insulators to find out which are the best and also the slimmest.

Handy Hint

☞ To test the insulating ability of small objects such as foam packing material, place all your bags and insulating materials in identical cardboard boxes or plastic tubs. Do the same if you want to test liquids such as water, rubbing alcohol, or dishwashing liquids.

Why-Oh-Why?

How does insulation work? Why are some materials better insulators than others? Check out page 74 for cool answers to some hot questions.

SLIM-SULATION TOO

Flora Fox's foxy fur coat keeps her warm all winter, but it sure takes up a lot of space in her closet. Is there something thinner that will keep her just as warm?

YOU NEED

⇒ 2 pull-tab aluminum soft drink cans

⇒ 2 glass or plastic, rigid aquarium thermometers (range: to about 40° C or 100° F or higher)

⇒ modeling clay

⇒ hot water

⇒ any material you would like to test as insulation, such as newspaper, cardboard, plastic wrap, aluminum foil, fabric, fake fur, a winter scarf or glove

Let's Experiment!

1. Some aquarium thermometers have suction cups at the bottom. Remove them.

2. Wrap one of the cans with the material you want to test. Leave the other can unwrapped.

3. Fill both cans with hot water.

29

4. Put the thermometers through the holes in the cans. Make sure the base of each thermometer is in the water.

5. Use clay to seal the tops of the cans and hold the thermometers in place. *You should be able to see the 20° C or 70° F mark above the clay.*

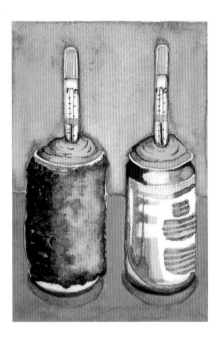

6. Read the temperature in the cans every ten minutes. After one hour, which can is warmer? Can you explain why?

Material	Temperature	
	Start	End
Hat	85	61
Cardboard	85	58
Newspaper	85	41
Wax paper	85	

Handy Hints

☞ The temperature inside the two cans should be the same when you start, but thermometers can vary. Make sure you read both and write down the numbers.

☞ Many aquarium thermometers have two scales: a Fahrenheit (° F) scale and a Celsius (° C) scale. Scientists always use the Celsius scale. You may use either one. Just make sure you don't mix them up.

See Handy Hints for Hot Colors, page 27.

WANT TO DO MORE?

⇒ Test many different materials to see how well they *insulate*. Make a table like the one above to compare them.

Why-Oh-Why?

How do animals stay warm in cold climates or seasons? How do people keep houses, food, and water warm? You'll be getting hot in your search for answers if you turn to page 74.

CUDDLE IN THE COLD

One cold winter's night, Billy Buffalo got mad at the others in his herd and decided he'd go it alone. Will he be sorry?

YOU NEED

⇒ 7 aluminum soft drink cans (pull-tab type, empty)

⇒ 2 glass or plastic, rigid aquarium thermometers (range: to about 40° C or 100° F or higher)

⇒ modeling clay

⇒ hot water

⇒ large rubber band

Let's Experiment!

1. Some aquarium thermometers have suction cups at the bottom. Remove them.

2. Fill all the cans with hot water.

3. Put the thermometers through the holes in two

cans. Make sure the base of each thermometer is in the water.

4. Use clay to hold the thermometers in place. *You should be able to see the 20° C or 70° F mark above the clay.*

5. Seal the tops of the other five cans with clay. Put them in a circle

Handy Hints

☞ The temperature inside the two cans should be the same when you start, but thermometers can vary. Make sure you read both and write down the numbers.

☞ Many aquarium thermometers have two scales: a Fahrenheit (° F) scale and a Celsius (° C) scale. Scientists always use the Celsius. You may use either one. Just make sure you don't mix them up.

around one of the cans that has a thermometer. Hold them in a circle with a rubber band. Leave the other can by itself.

6. Read the temperature in the cans every ten minutes. After one hour, which can is warmer? Can you explain why?

WANT TO DO MORE?

⇒ Would a bigger cuddle keep Billy Buffalo even warmer? Try more cans and see.

⇒ Does group membership pay off for a chilly buffalo, no matter where he stands in the herd? Measure the temperature in a can on the *outside* of the cuddle.

Why-Oh-Why?

Cuddling together in a group can help animals stay warm. Can you explain why? Cuddle up with some answers on page 74.

YODEL FOR YOGURT

"I scream, you scream, we all scream for . . . " WHAT? *The answer used to be ice cream, but frozen yogurt and other low-fat treats have become so popular that—in the United States today—about seven out of every ten scoops sold are the non-cream variety.*

Are you longing for a frozen yogurt, but all you have is the soft kind? How about making some that looks just like watermelon?

YOU NEED

⇒ 2 large oatmeal containers

⇒ 2 small bowls

⇒ 2 small cartons of plain nonfat yogurt

⇒ 2 tablespoons (30 cc) of sugar

⇒ ½ teaspoon (2.5 ml) of vanilla

⇒ 8 raisins (cut in half)

⇒ red food coloring

⇒ 2 sandwich-size zip-top freezer bags

⇒ waterproof marker

⇒ 2 gallon-size (4-liter) zip-top freezer bags

⇒ 16 large ice cubes

⇒ measuring cup

⇒ measuring spoons

⇒ mixing spoon

⇒ 5 tablespoons (75 cc) of salt

⇒ water

⇒ a friend to help, if possible

Pour the mixture into a sandwich bag and squeeze the air out. Seal tightly.

2. Repeat step 1 with the other carton of yogurt.

3. Use the waterproof marker to write "No Salt" on the outside of one of the gallon bags. Put eight large ice cubes and 1½

cups (375 ml) of cold water into the bag, along with one of the yogurt packets. Press out the air and seal tightly. *No leaks!*

4. Write "Salt" on the other gallon bag. Put eight large ice cubes and 1½ cups (375 ml) of cold water into the bag. Stir in the salt. Then add a bag of yogurt. Press out the air and seal tightly, with no leaks, just as you did before.

5. Roll the gallon bags into cylindrical shapes. Place one in each of the large oatmeal boxes.

6. Get a friend to help you. Shake the boxes for ten minutes or longer. (If you're yogurt-ing alone, shake one box and then

Let's Experiment!

1. Pour one small carton of plain yogurt into a small bowl. Stir in 1 tablespoon (15 cc) of sugar, eight raisin halves, ½ teaspoon (2.5 ml) of vanilla, and a drop of red food coloring.

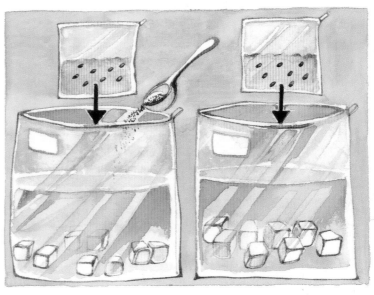

SALT   NO SALT

Handy Hints

☞ Be patient when shaking. The longer you shake, the firmer your yogurt will become.

☞ A rubber band around the gallon bags holds them securely inside the oatmeal boxes. There's less chance of a leak.

☞ If you don't have oatmeal boxes, try 3-pound coffee cans instead.

the other two minutes at a time for about 20 minutes total.)

7. When shaking time is up, open the bags carefully. What do you find? What's the difference between the two yogurts

now? What explains that difference?

WANT TO DO MORE?

⇒ Experiment to see if the amount of salt makes a difference in freezing time.

⇒ Make different colors and flavors of frozen yogurt. Try dried apricots with orange food coloring. Try lemon, almond, and peppermint flavors. What colors will you use?

Why-Oh-Why?

How can salt in ice water do what plain ice water can't? Shimmy on over to pages 74 and 75 to find out.

p a r t   f o u r

CRAFTY *Chemistry*

RUST BEFORE YOUR EYES

Hinges squeak. Wheels groan. Nails turn brown and furry. It's rust, and it shows up in all the wrong places—doors, cars, furniture, and appliances. Have you ever wondered what rust is or what makes it happen? Do some rust-proofing to find out.

YOU NEED

⇒ 5 shallow pans or dishes

⇒ paper, pen, and tape (for labeling)

⇒ 5 medium steel-wool pads

⇒ 5 fine steel-wool pads

⇒ newspaper

⇒ 2-cup (500-ml) measuring cup

⇒ water

⇒ measuring spoons

⇒ spoon

⇒ ½ cup (125 ml) vinegar

⇒ 1 tablespoon (15 cc) of salt

⇒ lubricating oil in a spray can

Let's Experiment!

1. Label your five pans: (1) "Oil" (2) "Water" (3) "Cold" (4) "Salt" and (5) "Vinegar."

2. Put one fine and one medium steel-wool pad on some newspaper. Spray both sides of each pad with oil. Don't miss the ends. Put the pads in pan #1.

3. Put two steel-wool pads, one fine and one medium, in each of the other pans.

4. Pour 2 cups (500 ml) of water over the pads in each

of pans #1, #2, and #3.

5. Dissolve the salt in two cups (500 ml) of water. Pour this over the pads in pan #4.

6. Pour ½ cup (125 ml) of vinegar mixed with 1½ cups (375 ml) of water over the pads in pan #5.

7. Put pan #3 in the refrigerator. Leave the others at room temperature.

8. Look at the pads after one hour. Can you see anything happening? Check again after two hours. Do you see any changes?

9. Leave the experiment overnight. Then observe the results and compare. What can you say about the effect of salt, vinegar, cold, and oil on rust? Does the size of the steel-wool strands make a difference? How can you tell?

WANT TO DO MORE?

⇒ Buy some iron nails at the hardware store. Put them in cups half full of various liquids. Observe the results after one week.

⇒ Keep a steel-wool pad submerged in water. What happens?

Handy Hints

☞ Disposable, aluminum, square cake pans work well.

☞ Touch the pads sprayed with oil as little as possible.

Why-Oh-Why?

What causes rust? What prevents it? When motorists complain that salt on the roads in winter rusts their cars, are they right? Turn to page 75 for some t-rusty answers.

Turn to page 75

SALTY SKATING

Chilly Billy wants to go ice skating this winter. Should he go to Utah to the Great Salt Lake, or should he travel to Ontario to skate Lake Erie?

Chilly needs to try this experiment before he decides. Would you like to help him?

YOU NEED

⇒ 2 plastic foam or paper cups

⇒ felt-tip marker

⇒ measuring cup

⇒ measuring spoons

⇒ 2 teaspoons (10 cc) of salt

⇒ water

⇒ spoon

⇒ freezer

Let's Experiment!

1. Write "Salt" on the outside of one of the cups. Write "No Salt" on the other.

2. Pour ½ cup (125 ml) of water into each.

3. Add the salt to the cup marked "Salt." Stir with the spoon until the salt dissolves.

4. Put both cups into the freezer.

5. Check the cups every 30 minutes for several hours. Do they look different?

6. Leave the cups overnight. The next morning, take them from the freezer. Let them sit at room temperature for about an hour.

7. Then turn them out in the sink. Do they look different? Poke them with a spoon. Do they feel different? Why?

SALT   NO SALT

WHAT'S NEXT?

Where are Chilly Billy's skating chances better—in saltwater or fresh? Skate over to page 75 to see if you're right.

AN ICY HANG-UP

Some nature experiments seem like magic, but there's a logical explanation. Amaze your friends with this one. Only you will know how it works.

YOU NEED

⇒ 2 plastic foam or paper cups

⇒ felt-tip marker

⇒ 2 ice cubes

⇒ 2 pieces of cord or heavy twine, each about 6 inches (15 cm) long

⇒ measuring spoons

⇒ ¼ teaspoon (1.25 cc) of salt

SALT   NO SALT

Let's Experiment!

1. Write "Salt" on one cup. Write "No Salt" on the other.

2. Put one ice cube in each cup. Wet the pieces of cord thoroughly and press them onto the tops of the ice cubes.

3. Sprinkle the salt over the cube in the "Salt" cup, covering the cord. Leave the other alone.

4. Wait a few seconds. Then lift the loose end of each cord. What can one of your icy hang-ups do that the other can't?

WHAT'S NEXT?

Are you hung up for an explanation? Turn to page 75 for some facts about freezing.

ONE-WAY WATERWAY

Potatoes may look lazy, but they're actually pretty busy critters. You can find out how.

YOU NEED

⇒ potato

⇒ knife

⇒ measuring cup

⇒ salt

⇒ water

⇒ 2 bowls

⇒ spoon

⇒ Way to Weigh scale (page 7)

Note: You need adult help for this one.

Let's Experiment!

1. Wash the potato. Ask an adult to help you cut two slices. They should be the same size and about ½ inch (1 cm) thick.

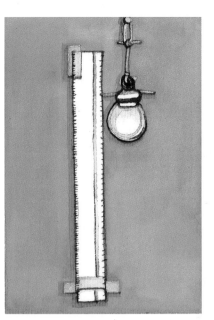

2. Weigh the slices on your Way to Weigh scale. They should weigh the same. If they don't, trim them until they do. Write down the number the toothpick points to on the ruler.

3. Put equal amounts of water into the two bowls.

Into one, stir salt until no more will dissolve. Label that bowl "Salt."

4. Put one potato slice in each bowl. Wait an hour.

5. Remove the potato slices from the bowls. Weigh them again. Write down the numbers. What's changed? Can you explain why?

WHAT'S NEXT?

Your bowls and potato slices are one-way waterways. Which way does the water travel in the bowl with the salt? How about the other bowl? It's a one-way trip to page 75 for answers.

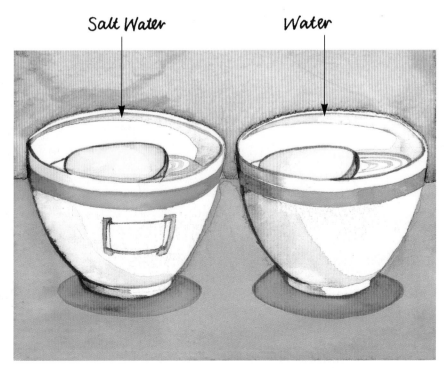

Salt Water   Water

THE SOUND OF
Music

· ·

A LIP-TICKLING TOOTER

What makes sound? This tooter gives a clue.

YOU NEED

⇒ drinking straw
⇒ scissors

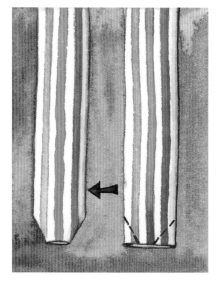

Let's Experiment!

1. Press one end of the straw flat and cut a notch on each side.

2. Make the cut end stay flat by pulling it between your teeth. Then push the straw firmly against your lower lip and blow down, as shown on page 41. Keep trying until you make a sound. What do your lips feel?

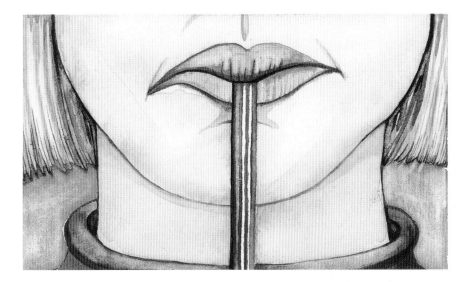

WHAT'S NEXT?

Try shorter or longer straws. Make finger holes in the straw. Try making high notes and low notes. Then turn to page 75 for some explanations that will be music to your ears.

THE BIG-NOTE BANJO

Everybody's moving to the music of the big-note banjos. Did you know that music itself is movement? You can show how by building and playing a big-note banjo.

YOU NEED

⇒ 27 disposable plastic cups
⇒ 6 identical rubber bands
⇒ yardstick or meter stick
⇒ nail file

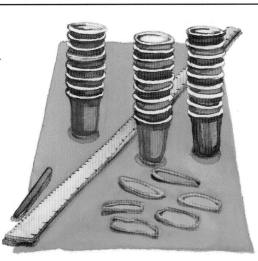

Let's Experiment!

1. Stack the cups inside one another—two in the first stack, three in the second stack, four in the third, and so on—until you have six stacks.

41

2. Put a rubber band around each stack.

3. Slide the stacks onto the yardstick, holding them in place with the rubber bands. Arrange the stacks from the smallest to the largest.

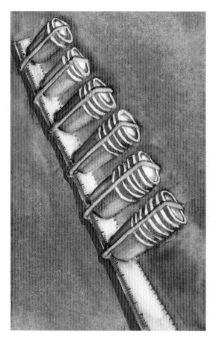

4. Pluck the "strings" with the nail file. Which stacks make the lowest tones? Which make the highest? Can you play a tune?

WANT TO DO MORE?

⇒ Push in on the sides of the cup while you pluck the strings. What happens to the PITCH (highness or lowness of the tone)?

⇒ Make a baby three-note banjo. Stretch three rub-

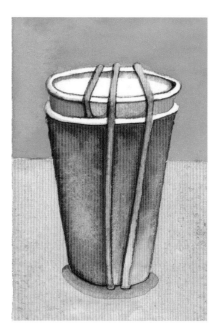

ber bands around two cups, as shown above.

⇒ Make a portable six-string banjo. Slide a rubber band around a stack of two plastic cups. Add a cup. Then add another rubber band. Keep adding cups and rubber bands until you have six strings in a stack of cups. Pluck with the nail file to play a tune.

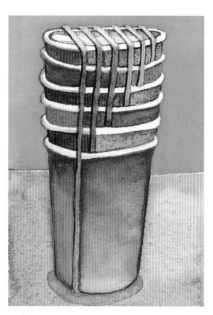

Handy Hint

☞ Keep the rubber bands straight and even. Twisted or crooked bands will spoil the pitch.

WRONG

RIGHT

Why-Oh-Why?

When you pluck the rubber band, you make a musical note. How does that happen, and what changes the pitch of the note? Dance on over to pages 75 and 76 to find out.

42

A WATER VIOLIN

This frog's tune is nothing but a croak. Can you do better?

YOU NEED

⇒ 3 or more glasses, same size

⇒ water

⇒ nail file

Let's Experiment!

1. Leave one glass empty. Fill the second half-full of water. Fill the third to the rim.

2. Lightly scrape the nail file along the rims of the glasses. You should hear different musical tones. You can make a different kind of sound by tapping the glasses with the file.

3. How does the amount of water in the glass change the pitch? (Does the tone go higher or lower?)

WHAT'S NEXT?

Set up enough glasses so you can play a tune. Why are the pitches different? You'll find a symphony of answers on page 76.

CHUCKLING CHARLIE

*W*hen Chuckling Charlie laughs, you'll laugh too.

YOU NEED

⇒ disposable plastic cup

⇒ piece of heavy string or cord, about 12 inches (30 cm) long

⇒ water

⇒ felt, yarn, buttons, and glue (optional)

Let's Experiment!

1. Ask an adult to punch a hole in the bottom of the cup.

2. Thread the string through the hole. Tie several big knots outside the bottom of the cup so the string can't pull through the hole.

3. Wet the string. Grasp the string inside the cup between your thumb and fingers. Pull down sharply, letting your fingers slide over the string. Several short, quick pulls will make a chuckling sound.

4. If you want, you can glue on buttons, felt, and yarn to make eyes, mouth, and hair for your Chuckling Charlie.

WHAT'S NEXT?

Are you wondering what the experiment is here? Try making Charlie laugh

when the string is dry, and you'll learn something about both sound and motion. There's even something to giggle about on page 76.

44

part six

MOVING ALONG

SPEED SKATING

Lulu's a champion roller skater, but Lily can never seem to get it right. It'll take a lulu of an experiment to put her on her feet.

YOU NEED

⇒ toy car

⇒ board or sheet of cardboard

⇒ book

⇒ measuring tape

⇒ surfaces for testing, such as carpet, sidewalk, kitchen counter, or corkboard

Let's Experiment!

1. Work on a smooth surface, such as a table. Put the book under one end of the board or stiff sheet of cardboard to make a ramp. Place the toy car at the top of the ramp. Let go.

45

2. The car should keep going past the bottom of the ramp. Use the measuring tape to measure the distance the car travels.

3. Repeat steps 1 and 2 twice more. Write down all three measurements. To find the average, add the three measurements together. Then divide the total by 3.

4. Build the ramp *always the same height,* but in different places so that the car runs onto different surfaces. Try floor, carpet, sidewalk, grass, or somewhere else.

5. Take three measurements on each surface. Find the average. Make a table like the one below.

6. What can Lily do to improve her skating? How do you know?

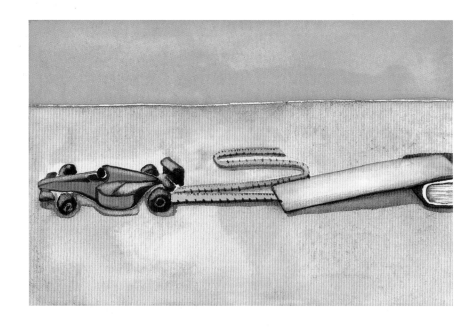

WANT TO DO MORE?

⇒ Set up three test tracks covered with sandpaper—coarse, medium, and fine. Does the grain affect the distance the car travels? Why?

⇒ Test different toy cars. Do some travel farther on the same surface than others? Can you think of reasons?

Handy Hint

☞ Be sure to start the car from the same place on the ramp each time you test.

Why-Oh-Why?

Why do some surfaces hold you back, while others send you spinning on your way? Skate over to page 76 to find out.

Surface	Trial 1 (cm)	Trial 2 (cm)	Trial 3 (cm)	Average (cm)
Table	65	72	66	68
Rug	31	26	-------	
Grass	-------	-------	-------	

WAY-OUT WALLOP

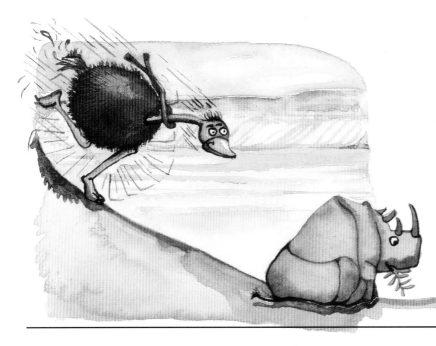

The rhino is about to find out what happens when an irresistible force hits an immovable object. Is he in for a way-out wallop? Here's how to find out.

YOU NEED

⇒ 2 rulers (one with a groove in it)

⇒ books

⇒ 2 marbles

⇒ index card, 3 × 5" (7.6 × 12.7 cm)

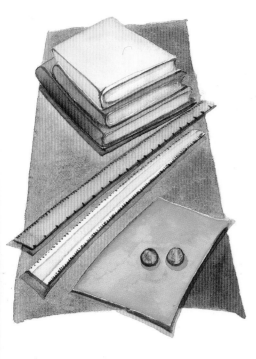

Let's Experiment!

1. Work on a smooth surface, such as a wooden table or floor. Fold the index card in half, then in half again.

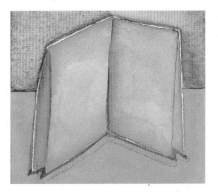

2. Put one end of the grooved ruler on a book. Put the index card at the bottom of the ruler, like this.

3. Place a marble at the high end of the ruler. Let

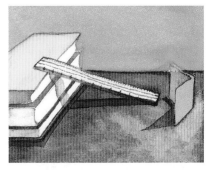

it roll down the groove and hit the card. The impact will move the card forward.

4. With your second ruler, measure the distance the card moved. Write the number down.

5. Repeat steps 3 and 4 twice more. Measure the distance each time.

6. Find the *average* distance the card moved by adding the distances together and dividing the total by 3.

7. Add a book to make the ruler higher. Repeat steps 2 to 6. Make a table for your numbers.

8. Keep adding books, rolling the marble, and taking measurements, until the ruler gets too steep for the marble to roll. What do your results show?

9. Now repeat the experiment, this time using two marbles released at the same time from each height. Make a data table as you did before.

10. How do the height of the ramp and the weight of the marbles affect the distance the card travels?

Height (cm)	Average Distance (cm)
10	26
20	35
25	44
30	

WANT TO DO MORE?

⇒ Keeping the height of the ruler the same, release a single marble from different points on the ruler. What do you notice about the speed of the marble and the distance the card travels?

⇒.Compare big marbles to small marbles without changing the height of the ruler. Does weight make a difference?

⇒ Put a brick at the bottom of the ruler. Put a marble in a toy car. Let the brick stop the car and send the marble flying. Does this experiment tell you anything about car safety?

Handy Hint

☞ If the marble knocks over the card, it's too close to the ruler. Move the card farther away.

Why-Oh-Why?

When a moving object hits something, it packs a wallop. Get up to speed and roll over to page 76 to learn more.

RUNAWAY RABBIT

*R*unaway Rabbit tries to run away, but he always comes back. You can build a Runaway Rabbit machine that does the same thing. Can you figure out how it works?

YOU NEED

⇒ 2 plastic-top cylindrical containers (like those that hold soft-drink mix tubs)

⇒ sharp knife

⇒ hole punch

⇒ scissors

⇒ rubber band, approximately ⅛ inch (3 mm) wide and 3 inches (8 cm) long before cutting

⇒ two ½-inch (1.25-cm) flat metal washers

⇒ drawing paper, crayons and glue (optional)

Note: You need adult help with this one.

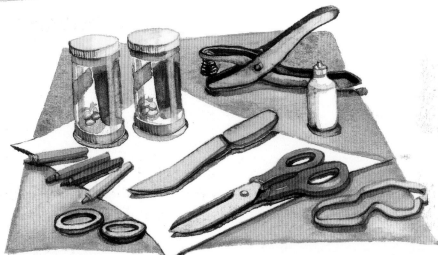

Let's Experiment!

1. Ask an adult for help with this part. Cut the bottom out of one of the containers with a sharp knife. Work the hole punch onto the lid. Punch two holes, one on either side of the lid. Punch two holes the same way in the other lid.

2. Cut the rubber band and thread it through the washers. Knot them securely in the middle of the rubber band.

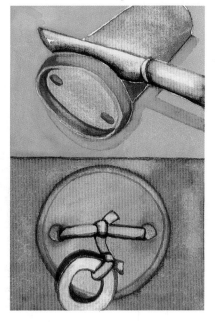

3. Thread one end of the rubber band through the holes in one of the lids. Work from the inside to the outside and back to the inside again. Tie the rubber band to itself inside the lid.

4. Repeat step 3 with the other lid and the other end of the rubber band.

5. Push one of the lids down through the cylinder and out the other side. Snap it into place.

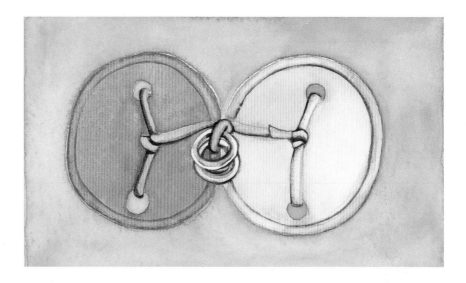

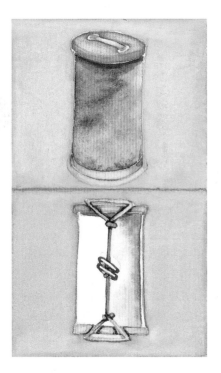

6. Pull the other lid back and snap it into place on the opposite end.

7. Put your runaway machine on a smooth floor or table. Roll it away from you. It should come back. If it doesn't, try a different rubber band, or try a fishing weight instead of washers.

Handy Hints

☞ After two or three tries, you may find that your rabbit stops coming back to you. Open the can, get the twists out of the rubber band, close the can, and try again.

☞ You can build a Runaway Rabbit from a different size of container, but you'll have to tinker with the length of the rubber band and the number of washers you use to get it to work.

WANT TO DO MORE?

⇒ Once your rabbit is working well, you may want to make it *look* like a rabbit. Cover the can with paper. Draw a face and tail on it.

Why-Oh-Why?

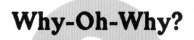

Runaway Rabbit is fun to play with, but there's a serious reason why it works. Can you figure it out? Roll over to pages 76 and 77 for Runaway's reason.

SHIFTY GEARS

*O*ne of these bicycling baboons is shifty when it comes to gears. Are you?

YOU NEED

⇒ cribbage board and pegs

⇒ spools, at least 3 the same size and 3 of different sizes

⇒ rubber bands

⇒ felt-tip marker

⇒ masking tape (optional)

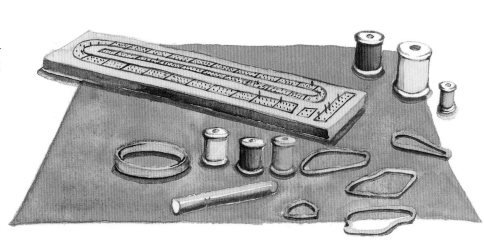

Let's Experiment!

1. Use a marker to draw an arrow on one end of each spool. If the spools are plastic, you may need to stick on a bit of masking tape to draw on.

2. Put two pegs in holes on the cribbage board. Put two spools of the same size on the pegs. Connect the spools with a rubber band. Point the arrows in the same direction.

3. Turn one spool one full turn. Watch the arrow on the other spool. How many turns does it make?

4. Now cross over the rubber band. What do you

think will happen? Try it and see.

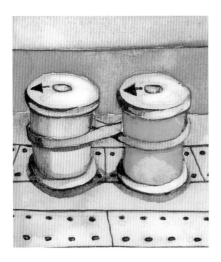

5. Replace one of the spools with a smaller one or a bigger one. Connect the spools with a straight rubber band.

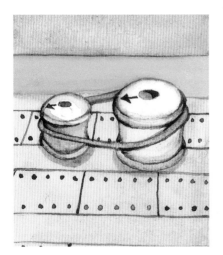

6. Turn the larger spool one full turn. How many turns does the smaller one make?

Handy Hints

☞ Keep the rubber bands low on the spools, so that they'll wobble less.

☞ Remove paper labels from the ends of spools. They can interfere with turning.

☞ If you don't have a cribbage board, ask an adult to help you build a base out of peg board and wooden dowels.

7. Try three spools arranged like this:

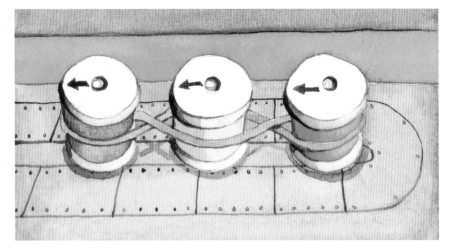

Or like this:

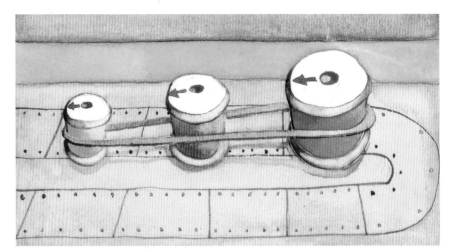

What happens?

8. Think up other arrangements to make and test.

WANT TO DO MORE?

⇒ Find and record the RATIO of one spool to another. Say, "For one turn of spool ___, spool ___ turns ____ times." Record your numbers.

Why-Oh-Why?

Interlocking wheels can change two things about motion. What are they? Roll on over to page 77 to find out.

For one turn of spool A, spool B turns 1 1/4 times.

For one turn of spool C, spool A turns 1/2 time.

For one turn of spool B, spool C turns 1 3/4 times.

Which spool is B?

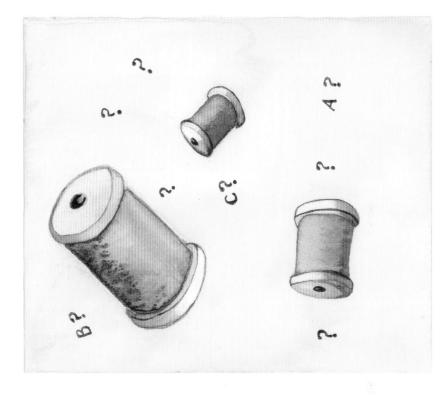

SOMERSAULT FOR SCIENCE

Sometimes things happen by chance. Sometimes they happen for a reason. How can you tell the difference? By counting, that's how. But first, you'll need to build a somersault machine.

YOU NEED

⇒ index card, 4 × 6" (10.1 × 15.2 cm)

⇒ hole punch

⇒ thin, stretchy rubber band

⇒ paper clip

⇒ tape

⇒ pencil and paper

Let's Experiment!

1. Fold the index card in half. Fold the crease back and forth several times to make it flexible.

2. With the card folded, punch a hole through both thicknesses about ½ inch (1.25 cm) in from the edge of the card opposite the fold.

3. Thread one end of the rubber band through one of the holes. Open it to make a loop. Push the other end through the loop. Pull tight.

4. Push the loose end of the rubber band through the other hole from the inside. Attach a paper clip. Without stretching the rubber band, tape the paper clip to the outside of the card.

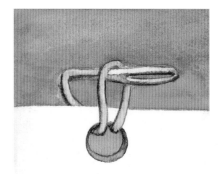

5. Write "A" on one side of the outside of the card. Write "B" on the other side. Label the insides the same way. This is your somersault machine.

6. Fold the card inside out. Set it flat on the table. Let

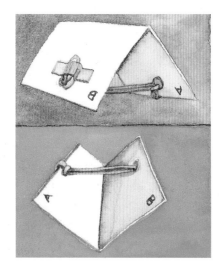

go. How does your somersault machine land? There are four possibilities:

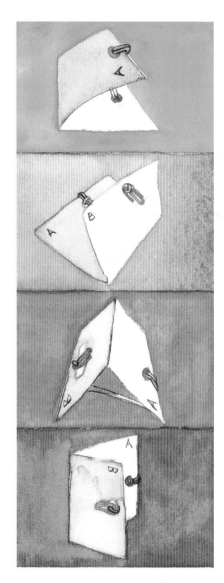

7. Release your somersault machine 50 times, starting with the "A" side up. Each time it lands, record its position. Does it come up more often one way than another? Do you have any idea why?

WHAT'S NEXT?

Do the experiment 50 times, starting with the "B" side up. Does the starting position make any difference? Flip on over to pages 77 and 78 to compare your findings to someone else's.

Flip on over to pages 77 and 78

part seven

LOOKING AT LIFE

FOOD FOR THOUGHT

All living things need food, but you may not be able to see them eat—not unless you're clever enough to look for the signs.

YOU NEED

⇒ 2 plastic lemons or limes, with dropper inserts and screw caps*

⇒ box of fishing weights

⇒ measuring cup

⇒ measuring spoons

⇒ spoon

⇒ 1 teaspoon (5 ml) of active dry yeast

⇒ 1 teaspoon (5 ml) of molasses

⇒ warm water

⇒ deep pot

*Note: Make sure your lemons or limes have removable plastic dropper inserts under the cap. The top should look like this:

Let's Experiment!

1. Make sure the plastic lemons or limes are clean and well rinsed. Ask an adult to remove the dropper inserts from them.

2. Count out enough fishing weights to fill each lemon about one-quarter full. Use the same number and size of weights in each lemon.

3. Fill the measuring cup with warm (not hot) water to the 1-cup mark. Add the active dry yeast. Stir until all the grains of yeast dissolve.

4. Carefully pour the yeast-and-water mixture into one of the lemons. Fill it all the way to the top. Put in the dropper insert and screw on the cap.

5. Add the molasses to the yeast-and-water mixture that's still in the measuring cup. Stir to dissolve.

6. Fill the other lemon with this mixture. Add the dropper insert and cap as you did before.

7. Set the lemons in the pan. Fill the pan with warm (not hot) water until the lemons are submerged.

8. Working underwater, remove the caps from both lemons.

9. Within 10 to 20 minutes, you should see something start to happen. What is it? Can you explain it?

WANT TO DO MORE?

⇒ Set up several lemons with different foods added to the yeast and water. Try table sugar, honey, corn syrup, or jelly. Use a stopwatch to count how many bubbles rise from each lemon in a minute. This will tell you which food helps yeast cells grow more rapidly.

⇒ Set up lemons with yeast and molasses in hot, cold, and warm water. Does temperature affect how fast the yeast cells eat?

⇒ Try adding other things to the yeast/water/molasses mixture, such as vinegar, lemon juice, salt, or baking soda. What happens?

Handy Hint

☞ If there are not enough weights in the lemons, they may start to float after a while. Hold them underwater. Remember to add more weights the next time you do the experiment.

Why-Oh-Why?

Did you realize that dried yeast is actually millions and millions of living yeast cells? How did this experiment tell you that the yeast cells were eating? Find some food for thought on page 78.

HOW DOES YOUR GARDEN GROW?

Growing plants is easy. Stick some seeds in the ground and the next thing you know . . . first prize at the County Fair!

"There's more to it than that," says Gary Gardener.

"There sure is," says Belinda Blossom.

Find out what they're talking about with this experiment.

YOU NEED

⇒ 4 shallow pans (small loaf pans work well)

⇒ 4 cellulose sponges (that fit inside the pans)

⇒ water

⇒ measuring cup

⇒ measuring spoons

⇒ ½ teaspoon (2.5 cc) of birdseed

Let's Experiment!

1. Put one sponge in each pan. In two of the pans, pour 1 cup of water over the sponge. Let the other two sponges stay dry.

2. Sprinkle ⅛ teaspoon (0.5 cc) of birdseed evenly over each sponge.

3. Place one wet pan and one dry pan in a bright, cold place such as a porch or patio (not the refrigerator).

4. Put the other two pans—one wet and one dry—on a warm, sunny windowsill.

5. Every day, check the water level in the wet pans. Add enough water to keep the sponges moist.

6. Every day at the same time, count the number of seeds that have sprouted (started to grow).

7. Make tables to keep track of your numbers.

8. After a few days, compare the plants that have sprouted. What differences can you see?

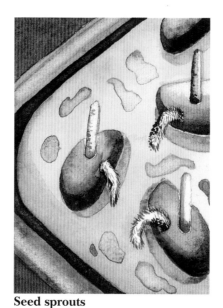

Seed sprouts

WANT TO DO MORE?

⇒ Experiment with the effects of water pollution on plants. Try adding vinegar, salt, dishwashing soap, or something else to the water in the pans. Compare your results with those using seeds sown in clean water. Can you see differences?

⇒ Investigate the effects of light. Try sprouting seeds in the dark and under a lamp.

Pan	Sprouts		
	Day 1	Day 2	Day 3
dry - light	0	0	
dry - dark	0	0	
wet - light	0	6	

Handy Hints

☞ If you can't find birdseed, use radish seeds instead.

☞ Don't use sponges with "scrubber" bottoms. They float. Clean, new, coarsely grained sponges work best.

Why-Oh-Why?

"Plants can't live without water," says Gary Gardener.
"Plants can't live without warmth," says Belinda Blossom.
Who's right? Why not plow your way over to page 78 to settle the argument?

A COZY POSY GREENHOUSE

Gardeners like to keep their posies cozy in a greenhouse. Try this experiment to find out why.

YOU NEED

⇒ 2 shallow pans (small loaf pans work well)

⇒ 2 cellulose sponges (small enough to fit inside the pans)

⇒ measuring cup

⇒ measuring spoons

⇒ water

⇒ ¼ teaspoon (1.25 cc) of birdseed

⇒ plastic wrap

⇒ rubber band

⇒ bright lamp (goose-neck is best)

Let's Experiment!

1. Wet the sponges and wring them out. Place one in each pan.

2. Add equal amounts of water to each pan until the water level stands about halfway up the sides of the sponges.

3. Sprinkle ⅛ teaspoon (0.5 ml) of birdseed on each sponge.

4. Cover one pan with plastic wrap. Seal it with a rubber band. Leave the other pan open.

5. Place the pans under a bright light.

6. Check the sponges every day. Add water, if necessary, to keep the level steady.

7. Every day, count the number of seeds that have sprouted. Make a record sheet for your numbers.

8. Do you see differences? Can you explain why?

WANT TO DO MORE?

⇒ Experiment with different materials. Try covering pans with waxed paper, glass, or clear vinyl. Does one work better than another?

⇒ Try covering the pans with colored cellophane or black plastic cut from a garbage bag. Does color make a difference in how soon the seeds sprout?

Handy Hints

☞ Don't let your sponges dry out or your seeds won't sprout.

☞ Use new sponges. Old ones that have traces of soap or cleaning products in them may kill seedlings.

Pan	Sprouts		
	Day 1	Day 2	Day 3
Covered	0	0	9
Uncovered	0	0	6

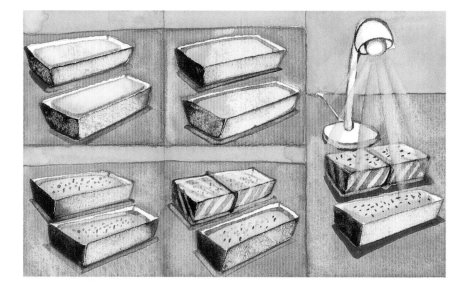

Why-Oh-Why?

The plastic wrap keeps the water from getting out. Can you see how? Is that all the plastic does? Mosey on over to page 78 for some answers.

UP, UP, AND AWAY

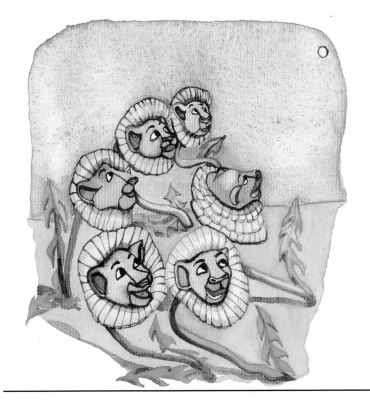

*I*t's summertime, and the grass is dotted with yellow dandelions. Here, there, and everywhere, the hardy golden blossoms turn their faces to the Sun. But hang on. How do they do that? How do dandelion stems know which way is up?

Do this DAN-dy experiment to find out.

YOU NEED

⇒ 4 clean, empty soup cans

⇒ 8 dandelion flower stalks *before* the blooms open

⇒ tall, narrow can, jar, or straight-sided vase

⇒ scissors

⇒ paper towels

⇒ 2 shoe boxes (or other supports)

⇒ water

⇒ tape

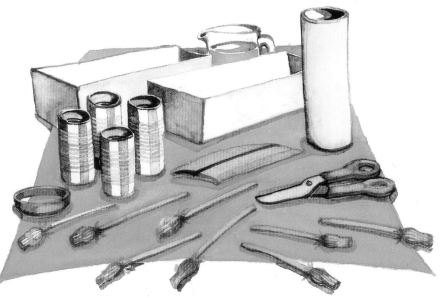

Let's Experiment!

1. Put a little water in the bottom of the tall can or jar. With scissors, cut eight dandelion flower stalks close to the ground. Select strong, sturdy stems at least 6 inches (15 cm) long. Make sure the flowers have not yet opened. Put the stalks in the can and keep them straight up until you are ready to experiment.

2. Soak paper towels in water. Squeeze out excess water. *In a darkened room,* turn the soup cans on their sides. Fill them half-way with damp towels, as shown. Then, carefully, in each can put the bases of two dandelion stems on the towels. Leave at least 4 inches (10 cm) of stem outside the can. Fill the rest of each can with damp towels, so that the stems are supported.

3. Snip the buds from the dandelions. Then turn the soup cans as shown. Use shoe boxes (or other supports) to hold one can upside down. Use tape to keep the cans from rolling.

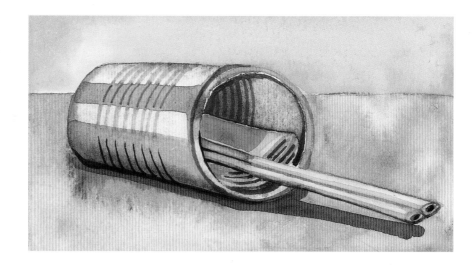

4. Wait and watch. Check your stems every 10 or 15 minutes for several hours. Draw any changes you see. Think of a way to explain what happens.

WANT TO DO MORE?

⇒ Dandelion stems have a "lag time." That's when nothing seems to be happening. Use a stopwatch to find out how much time passes before you see a change.

⇒ You'll get different results with stems of different ages. Compare results when you cut stems after the flower has opened, after it has closed, and after seeds have formed.

Handy Hints

☞ Handle the stems as little as possible before putting them in the cans. Keep the tall can or jar upright at all times.

☞ Cut stems carefully. Damaged stems won't work.

☞ If you can't find dandelions, try garden plants. Pansies work well, if a little slowly.

Why-Oh-Why?

Plants have no brains, so they can't know which way is up. Or can they? Angle your way over to page 78 for the scientist's explanation of what you have seen. (P.S. Can you guess why you needed to work in a darkened room?)

WORMING OUT OF IT

Ah, it's a worm's life! Nothing to do all day but crawl around in the soil. But, what's this? This worm is going to work. See him try to wriggle out of this one.

YOU NEED

⇒ 4 earthworms (see step 1 below)

⇒ pan (rectangular, glass or metal)

⇒ paper towels

⇒ jar

⇒ water

⇒ piece of black construction paper

⇒ tape

⇒ gooseneck lamp

⇒ thick book

Note: If at any time a worm quits moving or appears lifeless, stop the experiment immediately and return the animal to a grassy, moist spot. Keeping a worm out of its natural environment for too long can threaten its survival. All life is precious. Treat living things with respect!

Let's Experiment!

1. After a rain, earthworms often appear on sidewalks and driveways. Put some damp paper towels in a jar. Gently lift four worms from the pavement and place them in the jar.

2. Line the rectangular pan with damp (not soaking wet) paper towels.

3. Place one end of the pan on a table, the other on a thick book.

4. Put the earthworms in the middle of the pan, two facing toward the book, two facing away from it. (How can you tell which end is the head?)

5. Watch for a while to see what the animals do. Can they tell up from down?

6. Remove the worms from the pan. Take away the book so the pan lies flat.

7. Tape black construction paper over half of the pan. Place the pan under a strong lamp.

8. Put the worms in the center as you did before.

9. What do they do? Can they tell light from dark?

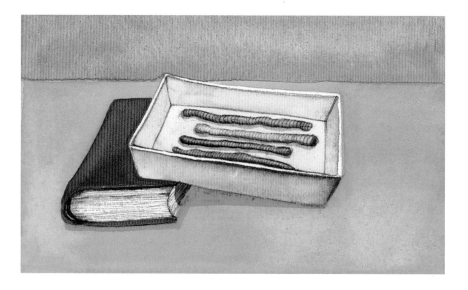

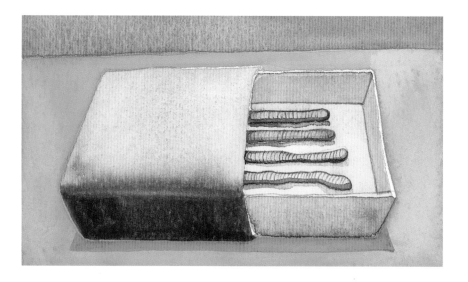

10. Take away the worms, the light, and the paper. Remove the damp paper towels from one end of the pan and replace them with dry towels.

11. Place the worms as before. Do they "prefer" wet or dry? How can you tell?

WANT TO DO MORE?

⇒ Try the same experiments with pill bugs (also called sow bugs), snails, or other slow-moving creatures. Turn over a rock or a log. You'll find them. Do they behave the same as earthworms?

Handy Hints

☞ Worms are like people. They don't all act the same. If you get confusing results on any of the experiments, try again later with more worms.

☞ Keep track of the total number that go to one side or the other until you begin to see a trend.

Why-Oh-Why?

Worms creep this way and crawl that way. But is all that creeping and crawling as pointless as it looks? Wiggle your way over to page 79 to find out which direction these creepy creatures crawl—and why.

p a r t e i g h t

THE EARTH

A SLANT ON SEASONS

Do you live in a place that has hot summers and cold winters? Have you ever wondered why the seasons are different? The Earth isn't closer to the Sun in summer, although many people think it is. Why, then?

Try this. Find a gooseneck lamp and turn on the light. Hold your hand directly under the bulb for a few seconds. Do you feel the heat? Now move your hand toward the side, so that the light still falls on your hand but not straight down. Feel the difference?

Now put your hand directly under the bulb again. Hold it there for a long time. Does it get hotter the longer you hold it there?

YOU NEED

⇒ 2 flexible temperature strips, or liquid crystal thermometers (sold in aquarium stores)

⇒ large piece of poster board

⇒ ruler

⇒ scissors

⇒ gooseneck lamp with bright bulb

⇒ pencil and paper

Let's Experiment!

1. Learn to read your temperature strips according to the manufacturer's directions.

2. Cut the poster board into a square by folding and cutting, as shown.

3. Find the center of the square by folding it in half each way, as shown.

4. Mark the center with a large dot. Then, along each of the fold lines, make a dot every 3 inches (8 cm). Number the dots 1, 2, 3, 4, and so on from the center. Label the lines "A," "B," "C," and "D."

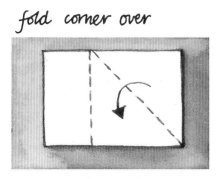

fold corner over

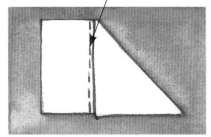

cut here

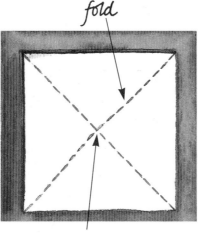

fold

center

5. On your paper, make a data table for recording temperatures, like the one on page 67.

6. Put the poster board under the lamp, with the bulb directly over the center dot. Put the middle point of one of the temperature strips over the center dot. Put another strip over any other dot of your choice. Wait a few minutes until the color stops changing on the strips. Then write the temperatures from the strips on your data table.

7. Take temperature readings at all the points, and

finish your data table. What do you notice?

WANT TO DO MORE?

⇒ Use string to measure the distance from the dots to the lightbulb. What do the different lengths mean?

⇒ Does it matter if the poster board is black or white?

⇒ Get a stopwatch and measure the effects of time on the temperature. Put a strip under the light and record the temperature every five seconds.

	A	B	C	D
1	82			
2		78		
3				
4				

Handy Hints

☞ If your lamp makes temperatures too high for your strips to read, raise the lamp.

☞ Stay away from breezes when you do this, and don't be in a hurry. Give the color plenty of time to settle on one number.

Why-Oh-Why?

What do gooseneck lamps and temperature strips have to do with the seasons? Get a slant on the seasons by turning to page 79.

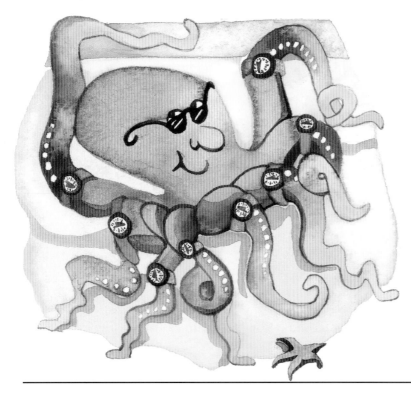

SUNSHINE, SUN TIME

Long before watches were invented, people used the Sun to tell time. You can, too, with this sunny-day experiment.

YOU NEED

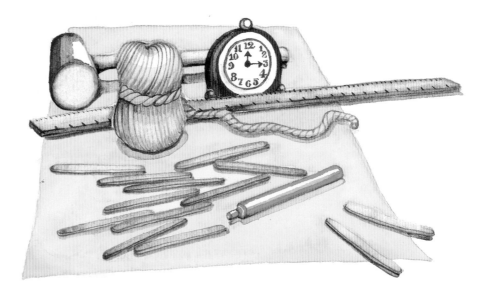

⇒ grassy, sunny plot of ground (no shade)

⇒ watch or clock

⇒ yardstick, meter stick, or wooden stake about 3 feet (1 m) long

⇒ hammer or mallet (optional)

⇒ ball of string or twine

⇒ 8 or more ice-cream sticks

⇒ felt-tip marker

Let's Experiment!

1. Set your alarm to get up early one morning—as early as the Sun does, if you can. Go outside and drive your stick or stake into the ground. (Pound it in with a hammer or mallet if the ground is hard.) Make sure your stake stands straight and solid.

2. Look at the time on your watch. Write the time on an ice-cream stick. Push the stick into the ground *at the end of the stake's shadow.* Tie a string between the stake and the stick.

3. Repeat step 2 every hour or so, all day long.

4. Make a drawing to record your results.

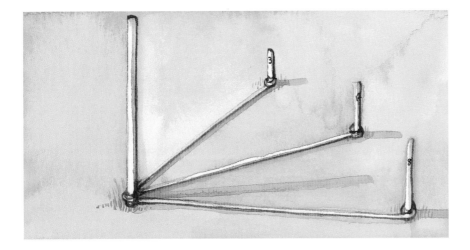

⇒ If you can leave your stake and sticks in place, wait a week or two and repeat the experiment, adding new ice-cream sticks and strings. Is your clock totally accurate?

⇒ Find our how real sundials work. How are they different from your shadow clock?

5. On another day, invite a friend to tell the time of day using only your shadow clock. Does it work?

Handy Hints

☞ If there's no grassy spot to work in, "plant" your stake in a pot or tall can, using soil or gravel to hold it upright. Make chalk marks on asphalt or concrete to keep track of the time.

☞ Watch out for trees and bushes at the edges of your plot. They may not interfere with your clock in early morning, but what about late afternoon?

☞ Your clock will be neater and easier to use if you add a stick and string every hour, on the hour.

"Look! From these sticks, I can tell it's 3 o'clock!"

Why-Oh-Why?

Does your clock become less accurate as the days go by? Can you explain why? Try the next experiment, An Angle on the Sun, to discover the reason. Then shine on over to page 79 to learn more.

AN ANGLE ON THE SUN

*T*he Sun is always overhead, it seems, in the sky somewhere. But is it in the same place every day? (Don't look at the Sun. You'll hurt your eyes.) You can find out in this experiment. You'll need a whole year to finish it, but be patient. It's well worth it.

YOU NEED

⇒ tall wooden stake

⇒ hammer

⇒ about 25 ice-cream sticks

⇒ permanent marker or a piece of chalk

Let's Experiment!

1. Find a sunny piece of grass where you can keep a stake and some sticks in the ground for a whole year.

2. Drive a tall wooden stake into the ground with a hammer.

3. Plan a day of the week and a time of day when you can check your stake

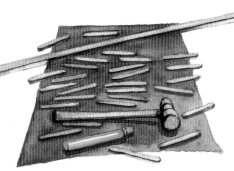

every two weeks. On the first day of your experiment, at the time you have chosen, mark the spot on the

ground where the *end* of the stake's shadow falls. Label an ice-cream stick with the date and drive it into the ground at that point.

4. Every other week, go back and do the same thing again. Soon you'll start to see a pattern in your sticks.

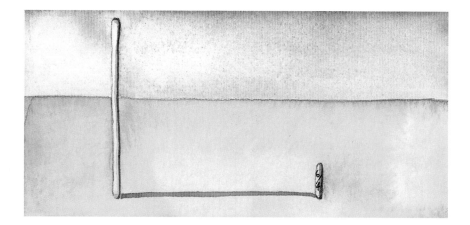

Handy Hints

☞ If the Sun doesn't shine on the right day, find the shadow's end a day or two later. Missing a few days won't hurt.

☞ This experiment depends on "sun time," not "clock time," so don't forget the change to daylight saving time in summer. If you are measuring at 3:00 P.M. in winter, "spring forward" to 4:00 P.M. after the time change. And don't forget to "fall back" an hour in the autumn.

☞ Be precise about the time you make your measurement. Even a few minutes can make a difference.

Why-Oh-Why?

What pattern did the shadows form on the ground?
Stake out the territory on seasons by turning to page 79.

Why-Oh-Why?

The Science Behind *Six-Minute Nature Experiments*

A Way to Weigh

Step on the bathroom scale and read the number. That number tells you two things. First, it describes the MASS (the amount of matter) of your body. Second, it measures the pull of the Earth (GRAVITY) on that mass. Weight is mass *multiplied* by gravity. Your Way to Weigh scale works because objects with greater mass (in the constant gravity of the Earth) pull the rubber band farther than objects with less mass.

Fun's A-Poppin'

Why did your popped corn weigh less, even though it took up more space? Unpopped corn contains water. When it gets hot, the water changes to steam. The expansion of the steam makes the corn pop. The steam escapes, and the corn loses the weight of the water.

That Sinking Feeling

Things sink or float because of the amount of space they take up (their VOLUME) *in relation to* their mass or weight. This relationship is called DENSITY. Density is calculated by dividing mass by volume.

We usually compare densities to water. Water, by definition, has a density of 1. That's because 1 cubic centimeter of water weighs 1 gram ($1 \div 1 = 1$). Things that have a density greater than 1 sink. Things that have a density less than 1 float.

What does your experiment tell you about the density of oil? Is it less than 1 or greater than 1? How do you know? What about the density of ground pepper and minced garlic?

A Cotton Tale

The two cotton balls have the same volume and very nearly the same weight. Their density starts out as less than 1. That's why they float. (See That Sinking Feeling.) The cotton ball that's coated with oil cannot absorb water, but the dry ball can. As it takes on water, its density increases, so it sinks. The oil-coated ball remains less dense than water and floats.

Boatloads

See That Sinking Feeling. Vegetable oil is less dense than water. Corn syrup is more dense.

When's a Boatful Not a Boat, Full?

See That Sinking Feeling. Freshwater has a density of 1, but the density of salt water is greater than 1. That means things floating in it are less likely to sink. They ride higher in the water, too.

All Puddled-Up

Pour some water through your hands. You are feeling

billions and billions of MOLECULES, or tiny "pieces," of water too small to see. These molecules are always moving. In a puddle, molecules moving at the surface sometimes escape into the air. That's called EVAPORATION. Your shallow puddle dried up faster because more surface was exposed to the air, so more water molecules escaped, or evaporated.

Rain, Man!

Water from the glasses evaporates into the air. (See All Puddled-Up.) When it hits a cold surface, it collects and becomes liquid water again, forming drops. Above the hot water, drops form on the bag and eventually drip off. That's rain. The same thing happens above the cold water, but so slowly that you don't see it.

Drops also form on the outside of the cold glass. That's water from the air becoming liquid when it collects on a cold surface.

The Freezin' Season

As you saw, water doesn't shrink when it freezes. It expands. That's because freezing causes the water molecules to line up in an orderly pattern with a lot of empty space between them. The molecules end up farther apart than they are in unfrozen water.

A lot of snow melts to only a little water. That's because the air between individual snowflakes takes up a lot of space.

Soap Boats

Some water molecules (see All Puddled-Up) escape into the air from the surface of the water. Others stay behind and tend to hold together. That's because they have slight electrical charges that attract one to another. This creates SURFACE TENSION.

Soap breaks the attraction and lets water molecules spread farther apart. That lessens the "pull" that the water molecules exert on the foil boat. When set free, the boat can skim across the water, riding a "wave" of reduced surface tension.

Wet, Wetter, Wettest

Paper towels absorb water for two reasons. First, water can move into the spaces between the fibers of the towel. Second, the fibers themselves take on water, because of their electrical, chemical, and physical properties. The more absorbent the fibers and the more space for water to move into, the more water the towel can absorb.

A Heat Wave

Water molecules (see All Puddled-Up) are always moving. They move faster when they get hot. When they move faster, they spread out and take up more space. When the water in the can gets hot, the fast-moving water molecules have no place to go but up into the straw, so the colored liquid rises. Cool the water, and the slower-moving molecules retreat back down into the can.

The Greenhouse Effect

When light shines into a greenhouse, it heats things up inside. The glass keeps the heat from escaping, so the greenhouse stays warmer than the air outside.

The Earth itself acts like a giant greenhouse. The Sun shines on the Earth, heating it. Gases in the atmosphere act like the glass in a greenhouse. They block heat from leaving.

When we burn fuel, run factories, or drive cars, we add extra gases to the air. Air pollution increases the greenhouse effect and may

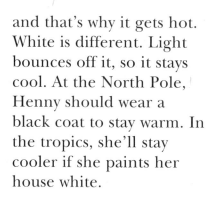

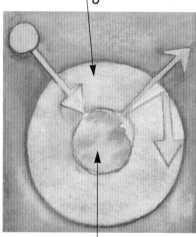

atmosphere

Earth

be warming our Earth too much. That could cause serious changes in our climate in the future.

Hot Colors

When light strikes a surface, one of two things can happen. It can be absorbed into the material or it can bounce off.

The more light a material absorbs, the hotter it gets. Black absorbs all light. None bounces back. That's why it looks black

and that's why it gets hot. White is different. Light bounces off it, so it stays cool. At the North Pole, Henny should wear a black coat to stay warm. In the tropics, she'll stay cooler if she paints her house white.

Slim-sulation One

The air is warmer than the ice cubes. That means the air molecules are moving faster than the ice molecules; that is, they have more ENERGY. As the air molecules move around the ice cube, some of that energy is transferred to the ice, causing its molecules to move faster, too. When they do, the ice warms and melts. Some materials are good at keeping the warm air away from the ice, so the ice lasts longer. These are good insulators. Materials that let energy pass through easily are poor insulators.

Slim-sulation Too

This experiment is the reverse of Slim-sulation One, but the science is the same. In this case, the fast-moving molecules of hot water inside the can have a lot of energy. Some of that energy is lost through the can to the air, so the liquid cools. A good insulator slows the loss of energy, keeping the water warm longer.

Cuddle in the Cold

Read Slim-sulation One and Slim-sulation Too. In this experiment, the cans on the outside lose more energy to the air than the one on the inside. The outer ones insulate the inner one.

Yodel for Yogurt

Because salt water freezes at a lower (colder) temperature than freshwater, a solution of salty water with ice is actually colder than ice. (Freshwater freezes at 0° C, or 32° F. Salty ice water can hit a low of − 18° C, or 0° F) Thus, a mixture of ice and salt water can gain more heat than can water free of salt. In the closed bag, the only place to absorb heat from is the yogurt. That's why the salt–ice-water mixture can freeze the yogurt, while the plain ice water cannot.

Rust before Your Eyes

Rust is that reddish brittle coating that forms on iron. (Steel contains iron.) Rust is a combination of the iron, oxygen gas (from the air), and water. Any-thing that gets iron, air, and water together makes rust-ing happen faster. Keep steel-wool pads dry and they won't rust, but get them wet in air, and the process begins immediate-ly. Lubricating oil prevents rust because it coats the iron and keeps it away from water and air. Cold slows rusting, as do vinegar and salt (although they may damage the iron in other ways). Salting the roads does not cause rust-ing, but when salt damages the protective coating of

paint on a car, rusting may begin on the exposed steel.

Salty Skating

Salt water is harder to freeze and easier to thaw than freshwater. Billy will be skating on solid ice if he skates his figure-eights on Lake Erie.

An Icy Hang-Up

On the surface of the ice cube, the salt causes a little melting. Then the cold of the cube causes the water to refreeze around the cord.

One-Way Waterway

Molecules (see All Puddled-Up) always move from where there are lots of them to where there are fewer of them. Think of people on the beach. Most will move away from the crowd to find a nice big space of their own.

In the salt water, there are *relatively* more water molecules *inside* the potato than outside, where a lot of molecules are salt. So water leaves the potato. The potato shrinks and loses weight. But in plain water, there are *relatively* more water molecules *out-side* the potato than inside. So water moves into the potato. The potato swells and gains weight.

● = water   • = salt

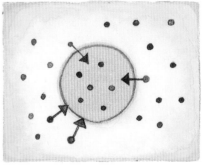

fresh water

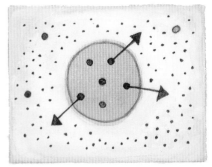

salt water

A Lip-Tickling Tooter

The vibration of the air and of the straw makes the sound. You feel the vibra-tion as a tingle on your lips. In general, longer straws make lower PITCH-ES (tones), but you can change the pitch by chang-ing the position of your lips or the way you blow the air.

The Big-Note Banjo

Pluck a rubber band and listen to the sound. Touch

the rubber band and feel the vibration that makes the sound.

To make the pitch of the sound higher, make the string shorter, thinner, or tighter. When you stretch the rubber band over a taller stack of cups, you make the strings both thinner and tighter, making the pitch higher. Press in on the sides of the cup, and you shorten the rubber band over the top of the cup.

A Water Violin

Scraping its rim causes the glass to vibrate. The vibration of the glass makes the sound. Water in the glass absorbs some of the vibration. The greater the amount of water, the less the vibration and the lower the pitch. An empty glass sings the highest note; a full glass, the lowest.

Chuckling Charlie

Sound is vibration. Chuckling Charlie's string vibrates when you slide your fingers along it. The cup vibrates along with the string and makes the sound louder. Dry string doesn't vibrate very well. The string must be wet to make Charlie chuckle.

Speed Skating

Try sliding the sole of your shoe along a rough surface, such as a thick carpet or grass. The surface seems to be holding you back, doesn't it? The "pull" you feel is FRICTION. Now think about what would happen on a slick surface, such as ice. Your foot would slide more freely, wouldn't it? That's because there would be less friction between your shoe and the surface. In this experiment, your car went farthest on surfaces that had the least friction.

Too much friction makes motion difficult. Too little can be dangerous. Imagine what happens when a car goes around a sharp curve. When the road is dry, friction holds the car on the road; but when it's wet or icy, the friction is less and the car may crash.

Way-out Wallop

You're riding in a car. The car stops suddenly. You feel your body thrown forward against the seat belt. If the car is traveling slowly, you won't feel much. But if the car is going fast, you can ram into your seat belt with a lot of force. That force is MOMENTUM. It is the mass of the object *multiplied by* its speed.

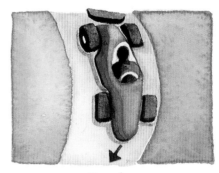

Friction

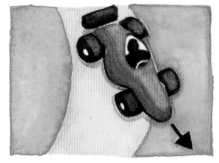

Less friction

In your experiment, you increased the speed of the marble when you raised the ramp. That increased momentum. When you used two marbles instead of one, you increased mass. That also increased momentum. Greater momentum made the card travel farther in both cases.

Runaway Rabbit

ENERGY is an idea we use to explain changes we can see or feel. When something changes temperature or moves, energy is either stored or released. There are several different

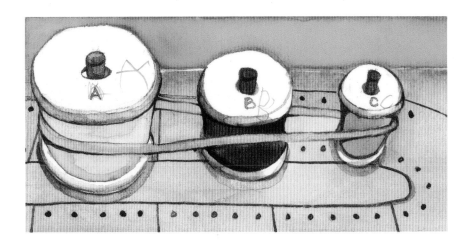

kinds of energy. KINETIC ENERGY is the energy of motion. Energy that is stored and may be released in the future is POTENTIAL ENERGY. One of the laws of nature is that energy is never created or destroyed. It only changes its form.

You give your Runaway Rabbit some energy (energy that came originally from your food) when you roll it across the table or floor. As it moves, some of that energy causes the washers to swing and twist the rubber band. Twisting the rubber band saves some of the rabbit's kinetic energy as potential energy. When the rabbit stops and the rubber band begins to untwist, that stored potential energy is changed back into kinetic energy as the rabbit returns to you.

Why does the rabbit stop rolling? Because some of its kinetic energy is lost to the environment as heat as it moves across a surface that exerts friction. See Speed Skating.

Shifty Gears

Gears pass motion from one part of a machine to another. They can also change the direction of motion.

If you ride a bike with gears, you know that the large front gear moves the bike fast, while you pedal slowly. Drop down to a smaller front gear, and you'll pedal faster, but the bike will move more slowly. Why is that?

When a small wheel is linked to a larger wheel, it must turn more times to move the same distance as the big wheel. That's why you pedal faster but cover less ground when you use the small front gear.

Look at the three spools on page 53. Can you see why A is the big spool, B is the medium spool, and C is the little spool?

Somersault for Science

The somersault machine is another example of potential energy being released as kinetic energy. (See Runaway Rabbit.) See some experimental results in the box below.

Here's what the experimenter concluded.
⇒ Starting with the paper-clip side up, the machine most often landed with that same side up.
⇒ Starting with the paper-clip side down, both sides came up with nearly equal frequency.

Starting position	Landed paper clip side up	Landed paper clip side down	Landed on long end	Landed on short end
Paper clip side up	38	8	4	0
Paper clip side down	17	24	7	2

⇒ Only occasionally did the somersault machine land on end.

⇒ It was more likely to land on end when starting with the paper-clip side down.

Your results may differ. How it lands depends partly on chance and partly on its design. The size and flexibility of the rubber band may affect the outcome, too.

Food for Thought

Yeasts are living things. Each grain of dried yeast contains millions of tiny yeast cells. When dried yeast dissolves in warm water and the yeast cells get some food (sugar), they begin to divide rapidly. One yeast cell divides and becomes two. Two become four, and so on.

Chemically, yeast cells break down the sugar in molasses. That process releases the energy the yeast cells use to grow and reproduce. Yeasts release a gas, carbon dioxide, as they break the sugar apart. It's that carbon dioxide that bubbles up through the water.

How Does Your Garden Grow?

Gary and Belinda are both right. Plants need both water and warmth, as your experiment showed. However, some plants are hardier than others. Some can live in the Arctic tundra, where it is both cold and dry. Others can live in the desert, where they withstand both high temperatures and water shortage.

A Cozy Posy Greenhouse

When light shines into a greenhouse, it heats things up inside. The glass keeps the heat from escaping, so the greenhouse stays warmer than the air outside. That makes plants sprout sooner. (See The Greenhouse Effect.)

Up, Up, and Away

Gravity is the attraction of one mass for another. The Earth is a big mass, so it has a lot of gravitational force compared to the small objects on it, like dandelions. Gravity is the reason the shoots of plants grow upward and the roots grow downward. Different parts of the plant respond differently to the gravitational pull of the Earth. But how do they do that?

Inside dandelion stems are some tiny bodies called AMYLOPLASTS. Amyloplasts are heavy capsules filled with starch and calcium. Calcium is the same

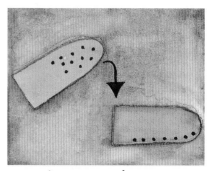

amyloplasts in stem tips

mineral that makes your bones and teeth hard. The amyloplasts act like stones. They fall to the bottom when the stem is turned.

Scientists know that the amyloplasts somehow "tell" the plant which way is down. But what makes the stem bend upward? It may have something to do with the positive charge that calcium IONS (charged atoms) carry. We know that plants in an electrical field can be made to grow in any direction. It seems that a charge affects growth. Maybe the lower side grows faster than the upper part, causing the stem to bend up, but no one knows for sure.

Why do you need to do this experiment in a darkened room? Because plants bend toward light, working in the near dark is the only way to make sure your stems are responding only to gravity and not to light. All the stems in the experiment are kept equally damp, so water can't be a factor either.

Worming Out of It

In general, earthworms will move down, away from light, and away from dry areas. This means their tiny brains must have some way of telling up from down, wet from dry, light from dark. Their movements make sense, considering how and where they live. Pull an earthworm from the ground, and it will burrow down again—away from light and dry air and into the protective moisture of its home in the dark soil.

A Slant on Seasons

The northern and southern halves of the Earth have seasons because our planet tilts on its axis. As our planet revolves around the Sun once each year, different parts are at different angles to the Sun. As you saw in this experiment, light rays heat things up more when they hit straight on than when they come in at an angle. So the half of the Earth that is getting the more direct (straighter) rays of the Sun has summer when the other half has winter. That's why it's barbecue time in New Zealand when it's ski season in Colorado.

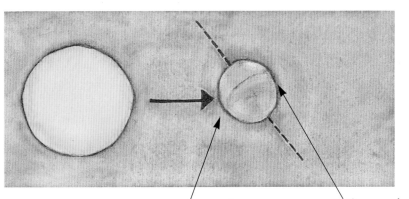

Summer in New Zealand

Winter in Colorado

Sunshine, Sun Time

As the Earth turns, the position of your stick *relative to the Sun* changes. In early morning, the Sun appears to be low in the eastern sky. At midday, it shines from more nearly overhead. As afternoon slips toward sunset, the Sun appears to move lower in the western sky. (Actually, it's the Earth that's moving, not the Sun, but the appearance is the same in either case.) As these changes happen, the shadow cast by your stick varies in its (1) length and (2) direction. By marking the end of the shadows at different hours, you record the time of day quite well. Your clock will grow less accurate as time passes, however. That's because the Earth changes its position in space relative to the Sun during its yearly revolution.

An Angle on the Sun

The lopsided figure eight that showed up on the ground reveals two things. First, the Sun is more directly overhead in sum-

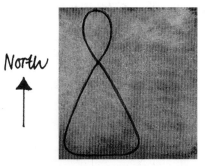

North

mer than in winter. The shadow your stake casts shows that difference in angle. Second, the 24-hour day that we use on our clocks is only an average. The length of a Sun-timed day varies from one day to the next as the Earth orbits the Sun.

Index